William Brewster

of the

Pilgrim Fathers

by

John Haden and the Pupils of
the Parish Church Primary School
Gainsborough

First published by Barny Books,
All rights reserved
Copyright © John Haden 2007

ISBN No: 978.1.903172.73.5

Publishers: Barny Books
              Hough on the Hill,
              Grantham,
              Lincolnshire
              NG32 2BB
              barnybooks@hotmail.co.uk

              Tel: 01400 250246

Copies of this book and the others in the ARIES series may be obtained from:

Julian Bower Associates,
Julian Bower House, Louth,
Lincolnshire LN11 9QN. UK
Tel: 01507 601254

Please enclose cheque payable to 'Julian Bower Associates' with your order and add £1.00 per copy to cover postage and packing.

See www.captainjohnsmith.co.uk for further details.

Contents

1. Four villages

Tucked away in a corner of northern England in the flat farmland where the counties of Yorkshire, Nottinghamshire and Lincolnshire meet are four small villages, Scrooby, Austerfield, Babworth and Sturton-le-Steeple. They are not important or impressive places, not much bigger today than they were four hundred years ago when something happened which led to the development of the most powerful nation in the today's world, the United States of America. People who believed that they were called by God into a special relationship with Him, left their homes to set out on a journey. It took them first out of England and across the North Sea to Holland and then across the Atlantic Ocean to the New World. Some called them the Scrooby Separatists but they are better known as the Pilgrim Fathers.

Most people in Tudor and Stuart England lived out their lives in the small world of the village in which they were born. Some had to travel as far as the nearest market town to sell the produce of their farms and bring back what they needed before night-fall. Some of the boys went to the local grammar school to be taught Latin, the language of all educated men right across Europe, and for a tiny number this would take them away from home into the wider world of commerce and government. What inspired these families to leave their homes was not a love of travel, a search for riches or a quest for fame. It was a search for freedom.

The Pilgrim Fathers were not the first to establish an English speaking settlement in America. Jamestown in Virginia was settled thirteen years earlier. But Jamestown was a business venture and a military camp for soldiers and explorers. Families came later. English men risked their lives on a venture which they hoped would make their fortunes when they found gold in Virginia and new trade routes to the riches of the East. They went as loyal subjects of King James and members of his Church of England. Eight out of ten of them died within a year of reaching Jamestown. Thanks to the energy and leadership of Captain John Smith of Willoughby in Lincolnshire, the colony at Jamestown survived, and eventually prospered when tobacco growing proved profitable. But few remember that Jamestown was the first.

The second settlement, five hundred miles up the American coast to the north-west, was at Plymouth Plantation where the Pilgrim Fathers made their home. They went together to find the freedom to live and worship as they chose and not as the Church and King demanded. Others joined their journey along the way. Many died not long after they reached their new home, just as those at Jamestown had died. Those who survived learnt to grow their own food, to live alongside the people whose land they came into and began to prosper as farmers and traders. They found freedom.

From these two roots, Virginia and New England, America grew. A string of coastal colonies came together as one nation, the United States, when they won their fight to be free from the English crown. In their struggle to expand across the continent from east to west, they all but exterminated the native American peoples whose lands they occupied. Eventually, Northern and Southern States fought a bloody war over another issue of freedom, the freedom of the black men and women brought to America as slaves. With the victory of the North, the Pilgrims' story displaced Jamestown as the story of the founding of America.

Many Pilgrims played their part in that story, but one man was a leader right from the beginning. His name was William Brewster and his home was in Scrooby, one of the four Pilgrim villages.

William Brewster's earliest days

William was born in Scrooby, England, in about 1567, during the reign of Queen Elizabeth I. His father was also called William Brewster and when William was about eight, his father got a new job, working for the Archbishop of York. He had to organise all the people who lived at Scrooby Manor and make sure that everything went well for the Archbishop when he came to Scrooby. The Brewster family lived in the Manor House. William's mother, Mary, died of the plague in 1586. His father remarried and had three more children with his new wife, Prudence.

(by Billy R.)

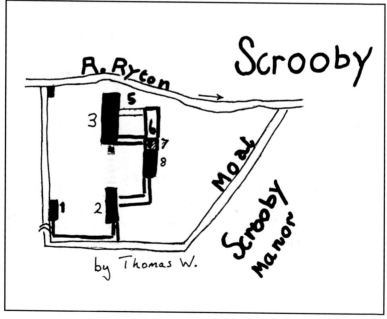

Scrooby Manor lies in the meadowland by the River Ryton on the edge of the village. The Archbishop needed a comfortable base from which to oversee the churches of the area and a well-run household in which to entertain his many guests. Margaret Tudor, the sister of Henry VIII, stayed at Scrooby on her way north to be married to James IV, King of Scotland and Henry himself came to the Manor in 1541.

The old timber and stone buildings were enclosed within a moat. Visitors coming from the Great North Road to the west, passed through the gatehouse (1) into the offices of the Archbishop (2) and along a gallery to the main building. This had guest rooms at one end (8), a chapel (7) in the middle and the Manor House where the Brewster's lived (6) at the other end. Another gallery linked this to the Great Hall (3) where the Archbishop could entertain his guests.

There were fish ponds and stables in the Manor grounds, and beyond the moat, the Archbishop's lands surrounded the village. By the Brewsters' time, the buildings were already old. Only one part of the Manor survives as a private house today but it is still one of the largest in the village. There are still horses grazing the surrounding fields.

The surviving part of Scrooby Manor House – now in private hands

Scrooby Manor from the best view point in Station Road

Our Life at Scrooby Manor

The oldest part of our home at the Manor was made out of stone but other parts were framed with wood. Scrooby Manor was a grand place to live because it was so big, like a palace. Poor people in the village lived in little two-roomed cottages but we had lots of rooms. Most of our furniture was made of wood. Mother and Father had a huge bed with a feather mattress, thick sheets and woollen blankets. We had wooden chairs and tables and the walls of the hall had wooden panelling with cloth hangings to keep the draughts out.

We ate beef and lamb, rabbit, pork and venison, and also wild animals like wolf and swan. We only used spoons and knives at meals, ate off wooden platters, and drank from cups made out of bulls' horns with the pointed end cut off. When the Archbishop came, there were big parties with lots of food and wine, jugglers and loud music.

(by Jason T.)

As well as his job as Steward to the Archbishop, William's father had another role. The Great North Road ran through Scrooby and the Queen's messengers carried important documents up and down from London to York and beyond to Scotland. (Our post is still called the Royal Mail.) All along the road, there were post stations where messengers could stay overnight and find fresh horses for the next stage of their journey. Mr Brewster was the Queen's Postmaster at Scrooby, paid to make sure that important royal messages got safely and quickly from Tuxford to the south to the next point in the chain at Doncaster, twenty-four miles to the north.

On the other side of the Great North Road from the Manor is the other large building in the village, the Parish Church of St Wilfrid. In the first thirty years of William Brewster's father's life, this Parish Church, and all the other churches of England, went through more change and upheaval in thirty years than in the centuries before and after.

When Henry VIII became king,. England was still part of the Church of Rome. The Catholic Mass was celebrated in Scrooby as it was in all parish churches. But when the King wanted to divorce his first wife, Catherine of Aragon, to marry Anne Boleyn, he broke from the Church of Rome and made himself Head of the Church in England. The church stayed Catholic and the Mass continued to be celebrated, but England was moving towards the Protestant faith. When Anne gave Henry a daughter, the future

Elizabeth I, and not a son, Henry tired of her too. She was accused of adultery and beheaded as a traitor.

The Parish Church of St Wilfrid, Scrooby

As he was now head of the Church, Henry could shut down the great religious monasteries, confiscate their wealth and sell off their property to his supporters. The men of Lincolnshire rose in anger against the King and soon a great rebellion spread across the North. It was called the Pilgrimage of Grace and the rebels came close to overthrowing the King. Church communities were dragged into this conflict and some parish priests lost their lives when the rebellion failed. Henry married again and his third wife, Jane Seymour, gave him at last what he most wanted, a son. Sadly, the queen died soon after Prince Edward was born but Henry had an heir.

Henry remained Catholic until his death, although he married three more wives. Anne of Cleves was divorced as soon as possible when Henry discovered that she was not as beautiful as her flattering portrait suggested. Catherine Howard was young and pretty. She accompanied Henry when he visited Lincoln and York and must have been with him when he visited Scrooby Manor in 1541. But she was so bored with her old and overweight husband that she took young lovers into her bed and paid the price with her life.

Finally, Henry married Catherine Parr, a motherly widow who met Henry's need for a nurse and a stepmother for his children. She had many Protestant friends and arranged for Edward to be brought up as a Protestant. When he became king as a boy of nine, his strongly Protestant Church of England was led by Thomas Cranmer. Church services changed from the Latin Mass to follow Cranmer's new English Prayer Book. But Edward died after only six years as king, and his Catholic sister, Mary, took England back into the church of Rome. For the next five years, Protestants were persecuted. Many fled to Protestant parts of Europe like Holland and Geneva. Cranmer and other Protestant leaders left in England were arrested, tried and burnt at the stake as heretics. For the five years of 'Bloody Mary's' reign, all of England had to worship according to the Latin Mass, or suffer.

When Elizabeth I came to the throne, she was determined to end all this turmoil and return England to a Protestant faith with a Prayer Book which gave order to worship and avoided extremes. But she did not believe in choice in matters of religion. When William Brewster was growing up at the Manor, all the villagers of Scrooby were required by law to worship at St Wilfrid's Church every Sunday. If you missed a service, your absence would be noticed and recorded. Those who made a habit of staying away faced fines and even imprisonment for defying the law.

2. Going to Cambridge

On a late autumn morning in 1580, two riders set off on a long journey south. The Queen's Postmaster at Scrooby Manor, was taking his son William to enrol in the oldest College in the University of Cambridge. They took the Great North Road, the main road to London from the North. With the rains of early winter, it was a muddy track deeply rutted from the wheels of farm carts and churned up by the hooves of cattle and horses.

The long road to Cambridge

William was already nervous as he and his father travelled south. What would the other boys be like, the students he had never seen before who were already at the University? In those days, travel was dangerous and you had to watch out for robbers lying in wait on the loneliest stretches of the road. They might jump out of the bushes and shout 'Stop! Give me everything you've got, your money and your jewelry.' William and his father must have been glad to reach the safety of a town before it got dark each night and the warmth of an inn to stay at.

(by Ben C.)

They crossed the wild places of Barnby and Markham Moors without mishap. The road took them past the great Forest of Sherwood, where Robin Hood had lived many years before. Even with changes of horses, it took them several days of riding. After Grantham, they followed Ermine Street, the straight road which the Romans built to take their marching legions quickly to the north. From Stamford, the Brewsters followed another Roman road across the flat Fens to Cambridge.

William father left him there to be admitted to Peterhouse, the oldest College in Cambridge University. The admission register still shows his name and the fact that he 'matriculated' or entered the College as a 'pensioner' on December 3rd 1580. His father was rich enough to pay for the boy's board and lodging, rather than enter him as a 'commoner', a student who would have to earn his keep by serving other students and members of the College.

Peterhouse was named after an old church, St Peter without Trumpington Gate. The students and fellows used this church as their first College Chapel when the Bishop of Ely decided that a small group, 'a Master and fourteen worthy but impoverished fellows', would live and study together. This tiny community became the model for all future Cambridge colleges. A hall was built for them to take their meals together and they met for worship in the little church, sharing it with the people of the town. Their community became known as the House of St Peter and eventually, Peterhouse, but never 'Peterhouse College'.

Life at Peterhouse had changed little since its founding and for William Brester it must have been more like a boarding school than a university today. Scholars had to swear an oath to uphold the good of the College. They had to wear clean clothes and behave well. They must not interrupt when anybody else was speaking and could only meet their friends in respectable places. The students were boys of twelve to seventeen, still very much under the authority of their parents, the College Fellows and the Church. At Peterhouse, each day began at 5 am in summertime and 6 am in winter with prayers in the Church of St Peter.

Peterhouse Hall, part of which dates from the 13th Century

Peterhouse hall where Brewster took his meals is still there. The church which was their chapel is also there, but it is now called Little St Mary's, tucked away in a railed-off churchyard on a corner of Trumpington Street. Inside, it is more like a College hall than a church, and there is a monument to the 'Rev. Mr Godfrey Washington, Minister of this church and Fellow of St Peter's Colledge, born 1670, died 1729'. Above the inscription, the coat of arms of the Washington family, three stars above two red stripes, is topped off with a rather splendid eagle. Godfrey was the great uncle of the young Virginian surveyor and soldier who became the commander of the American rebels against King George III and the first President of the United States. George Washington's family arms found their way into the Stars and Stripes. But within the church, there is no mention of the fact that William Brewster must have worshipped there when he was a student at Peterhouse.

The nave of St Mary the Less which was previously St Peter without Trumpington Gate where Brewster worshipped as a student

Brewster left no other trace at Cambridge and did not take a degree, but while he was there, the University was a centre of religious change. Elizabeth appointed two Cambridge scholars, Matthew Parker to be her Archbishop of Canterbury, and William Cecil to be her chief adviser. Between them, they worked out a new religious settlement in which England would be Protestant, but not extremely so. After all the years of religious turmoil, Elizabeth and her advisers found a middle way which brought stability to her realm.

Great St Mary's Church where Thomas Cartright lectured

Not everyone was content with this middle way. The greatest Cambridge scholar of his day, Thomas Cartwright, taught that the Church of England was only 'half-reformed'. His lectures in Great St Mary's Church were so popular that the windows had to be taken out so that the crowds standing outside could hear him. Cartwright studied the Book of Acts in the New Testament and taught that there were no Bishops in the early church. The first Christians in the towns of the Roman Empire met together to worship and were led by those who knew most about what Jesus had taught. They governed themselves as congregations without authority imposed from outside.

Cartwright's teaching influenced many at Cambridge. Brewster's own ideas about church organisation stem from his time there. Cartwright soon got into trouble when he was invited to debate the issues of authority in the Church with the Archbishop of York in front of Queen Elizabeth. He argued that the sovereignty of God did not need the support of kings and queens. Such views were dangerous. When he continued to denounce the role of Bishops in the Church of England, Elizabeth and her advisers decided that he had to be silenced. He was sacked from his university post and driven into exile in Geneva. But his teaching influenced many at Cambridge and started a movement to fully reform, or 'purify' the Church of England from within. The leaders became known as 'Puritans'.

Some wanted to go even further and leave the church of England altogether, to 'separate themselves' from a church they thought could not or would not be 'purified'. Young men studying at Cambridge with Brewster became the leaders of these 'Separatists', including John Penry, whose name is on the Peterhouse register with Brewster's, and John Greenwood who studied at Corpus Christi College. Both Penry and Greenwood were arrested for being Separatists, and both were executed, Greenwood hanged for sedition and Penry hanged, drawn and quartered as a traitor.

Another Separatist, Robert Browne, fled to Holland to escape arrest. His followers became known as 'Brownists' a title used against Brewster and his friends when they too moved away from the Church of England. But during his time at Cambridge and the years immediately afterwards, Brewster kept out of trouble.

3. Serving the Queen

After he left Cambridge, Brewster joined the household of William Davison, a rising star in Queen Elizabeth's service. How they met, we can only guess, Davison may have come through Scrooby on his journeys to the north for the Queen. He was a Puritan sympathiser and worked at the heart of Elizabeth's court. Davison soon found that young Brewster could be trusted.

Letter to my father at Scrooby Manor
1588

Dear father

I have just finished university and now have a job as a secretary for William Davison. We have been sent to Holland by the Queen to arrange her help for the Dutch. They are fighting the Spanish because they want to be independent. Queen Elizabeth 1 has sent out a large army to help the Dutch but she has made them hand over the keys to two of their towns, Brill and Flushing. I have the job of looking after the keys so I hide them under my pillow at night for safe keeping.

From your loving son,

William Brewster

(By Georgia R and Charlotte W)

The Spanish sent an army of occupation into Holland in the year that William Brewster was born. The Dutch tried to negotiate a peace but the Spanish would not listen to 'beggars'. Twelve thousand Protestant Dutchmen were condemned to death. The Dutch leader, William the Silent, began a rebellion against the Spanish. Without an army, his sailors formed a fleet which they called the 'sea-beggars' and attacked the Spanish-held towns. Their first victory was at Brill, the fortified town which contols the mouth of the River Maas. They then freed other towns and cities, including Flushing, Leyden and Delft, and formed the United Provinces of Holland. But William the Silent was murdered in Delft in 1584, leaving the Dutch without a strong leader.

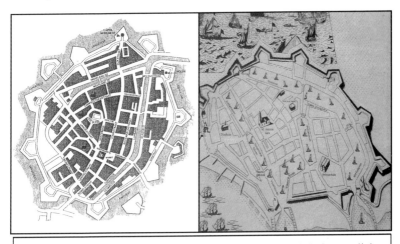

The Dutch 'cautionary towns', Brill and Flushing which the English army held after the Dutch liberated them from the Spanish.

They appealed to the English Queen, Elizabeth I, for help and even offered her their crown, but she was cautious and would only promise them the help of an English army. Even then, the Dutch had to agree to give the English the keys to Brill and Flushing so that the English controlled the rivers which ran into the heart of Europe, the Maas and the Schelde. The English called them the 'cautionary towns' as they held them as security against the loan of their army. Brill, now Brielle, still has the fortifications and defensive canals which Brewster would have seen when he rode with Davison at the head of the English army through the gates to receive the keys,

The Dutch were grateful to Davison and he returned to London with a fine gold chain in recognition of his efforts to help them. Brewster looked after the chain for Davison and was told to wear it when they rode in triumph through the streets of London. Brewster came back to England with experience of travelling and working in Holland and good contacts with the Protestant Dutch in their cities of Amsterdam, Leyden, and Delft.

But Elizabeth was angry, not at first with Davison but with her favourite, the Earl of Leicester. He had been sent to Holland as her General but had gone behind her back He accepted from the Dutch the very thing that she, as Queen, had refused to consider, overall control of the free parts of Holland. Elizabeth was even more jealous when Leicester and his wife were treated by the Dutch as if they were the king and queen of Holland.

When Davison returned to London bringing a letter to the Queen from Leicester, she refused to read it or even speak to him. Eventually she calmed down and when the dust had settled and her affections had moved to her new favourite, Leicester's son, Essex, she promoted Davison to be her Secretary of State. With his rise, his own secretary, William Brewster, came further into the machinery of government and into the next crisis of Elizabeth's long reign. What should be done about that unhappy lady, Mary, Queen of Scots?

Mary, Queen of Scots by Daisy R.

The Execution of Mary Queen of Scots

Queen Elizabeth was a Protestant and Mary Queen of Scots was a Catholic. Protestants and Catholics did not get on at that time. When the Scots decided to have Mary's baby son, James, as king, Mary fled from Scotland, hoping to get support from Elizabeth in England. But when Mary reached England, Elizabeth decided to keep her under arrest. For eighteen years, she was imprisoned, guarded by George Talbot, Earl of Shrewsbury, and his wife, Bess of Hardwick.

Elizabeth discovered that Mary was plotting with other Catholics to have her killed so that Mary could take over her throne. Mary hoped to get help from the French *and the Spanish who wanted to see a Catholic Queen in England. Elizabeth could not decide what to do, but she could no longer tolerate Mary's behaviour.*

Elizabeth finally agreed that Mary would be put on trial. She was found guilty of treason and sentenced to death. William Davison was told to draw up the warrant for Elizabeth to sign, so that the sentence could be carried out but Elizabeth could not bring herself to sign the document. She remembered that her own mother, Ann Boleyn, had been executed by her father, Henry VIII, and she did not want to be responsible for a Queen's death, especially as Mary was her relative as Henry's grandchild.

She even tried to arrange with Sir Amias Paulet who was guarding Mary to cause Mary to have a little accident to remove her quietly but Sir Amias refused to kill Mary. Eventually, William Davison arranged for Elizabeth to sign the warrant. Mary, Queen of Scots, was beheaded at Fotheringay Castle on February 5th1587. The executioner made a mess of the job and had to use three chops of his axe!

When Elizabeth was told of Mary's death, she was furious with Davison. She claimed that he had tricked her into making a terrible mistake and turned against him. For a time, his life too was threatened, but Elizabeth decided to imprison him in the Tower of London until she had calmed down. In the Tower, he did not need a Secretary.
(by Kaya W. and Jo B.)

Without a job to support him in London, and with Davison in disgrace, William Brewster had no choice but to leave the glamour of the Queen's service to go home to Scrooby and start life again in a rural back-water.

4. A new way to worship

Back at Scrooby, William Brewster helped his father as Bailiff and Postmaster. In 1588, he would have heard the great news of the defeat of the Spanish Armada from messengers travelling up and down the country. He might have had a chance of rejoining Davison when the Earl of Leicester died and the Earl of Essex became the Queen's new favorite. Davison was quietly released from the Tower but not given an important role at court. Brewster stayed at Scrooby.

By 1590, William's father was too old and sick to work and his son had taken over most of his duties. When his father died, William petitioned the official who controlled state appointments to take over the Postmaster role officially. With a little help from William Davison, still respected if not in power, Brewster was appointed to the two jobs he was already doing, serving both the Queen and the Archbishop of York. He was also quietly supporting not just the local Puritan Clergy, but also those with strong Separatist tendencies. William got married at this time and started a family with his wife, Mary, who shared his interest in religion. They called their first son, Jonathan, born in 1593.

It seems that the Brewsters kept their Puritan and Separatist views to themselves for several years, worshipping at their parish church while quietly developing a network of like-minded believers in the nearby villages. Six years after Brewster had gone to Peterhouse in Cambridge, Richard Clyfton, from Normanton in Derbyshire became the minister of the parish church of All Saints, in the nearby village of Babworth. Clyfton had also studied at Cambridge and the memorial plaque in the church records that his congregation 'became Separatists in May 1586'.

Clyfton's influence and preaching led them further down that road although he remained as their Minister. He married Anne Stuffen of Worksop and they raised a family of six children. When the Bishop's officers came to Babworth, perhaps sympathetic local gentry who shared his preference for Puritan theology and Separatist sympathies, protected him from getting into trouble.

Richard Clyfton's church at Babworth by George M.

Richard Clyfton was a good preacher and his sermons began to attract worshippers from a wide area. Amongst them were William Brewster from Scrooby and a young farmer's son, William Bradford, who was baptised as a child in the little stone church of St Helena's, Austerfield in March 1589. Bradford's parents died when he was a child and he was brought up by his uncles. He got to know the Brewsters at Scrooby and began a friendship with William which would last their lifetime. William Bradford looked up to Brewster as a father-figure and learned to love good preaching and clear Christian teaching. Much of what we know about William Brewster comes from William Bradford's book about the Pilgrim Fathers 'Of Plymouth Plantation'.

St Helena's Parish Church, Austerfield, where William Bradford was baptised

Together they walked to Clyfton's services at Babworth and although Bradford's uncles tried to discourage him, William continued to worship with Brewster. In spite of his Separatist views, Clyfton remained undisturbed for a time, but when the old Queen died, King James of Scotland became King of England and decided to tackle the problem of the Puritans.

King James and the Puritans

When King James came to the throne, he decided to keep England Protestant as Elizabeth had done. Both Catholics and Puritans had been prevented from worshipping in their own way. They were forced to worship in their parish church using the Prayer Book. The Puritans hoped that James would allow them to have simpler forms of worship. They did not want statues or stained glass windows or special long cloaks for their ministers in churches. They also believed that they should hold their own services without an ordained priest. But James made them conform and some of their ministers were sacked from their churches.

(by Ben N.)

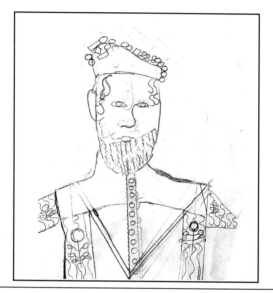

James VI of Scotland and I of England by Lucy E.

King James and the Bible

Henry VIII had the Bible translated into English so that it could be used in all the parish churches, but this old translation contained mistakes and the old-fashioned writing made it hard to understand. People known as Puritans during Elizabeth's reign wanted to make church services simpler. They lived strict lives, working hard and dressing plainly. The Puritans preferred the version of the Bible called the Geneva Bible. It had been translated by a group of Englishmen who had gone into exile in Geneva when Mary was Queen and persecuted Protestants. This version was very anti-Catholic.

James I disliked the Puritans. At the start of his reign, he asked a group of scholars to make a new translation of the Bible which everyone could use. The new bible came out in 1611 and most people felt that the language was clear and beautiful. The King James Bible has been reprinted many times since then, even though many newer translations exist.

(by Jack H.)

When King James met with the Bishops and the Puritans at the Hampton Court Conference in 1604, the Bishops were told to make sure that Church of England ministers used the Prayer Book. If they did not follow the rules, they would be kicked out of their churches. Richard Clyfton was one of the most committed Puritans in his area and in that year, he was evicted from All Saints, Babworth. For a time, William Brewster provided Clyfton and the Babworth congregation with a place to worship at Scrooby Manor where they were joined by another evicted Puritan Minister, John Robinson of Sturton-le-Steeple.

He had also studied at Cambridge and became a Fellow of Corpus Christi College. But he wanted to marry his sweetheart and had to resign from his fellowship to get married. He too had become a leading member of the Separatist movement. When he left Cambridge, he became the Vicar of Mundford in Norfolk but soon had to leave because the Church Wardens objected to his radical preaching. He ministered briefly at St Andrew's Church in Norwich, but lost that job when the Bishop of Norwich took away his licence to preach. He joined Brewster and Clyfton at Scrooby.

John Robinson's home church at Sturton le Steeple, now surrounded by the power stations of the Trent Valley.

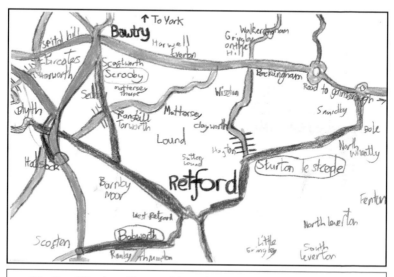

The four Pilgrim villages of Scrooby, Austerfield, Babworth and Sturton le Steeple, near the towns of Bawtry, Retford and Gainsborough   by Alex S.

Not far away, in the Market town of Gainsborough, another illegal Separatist Church had been established. The magnificent 15th Manor House, known as Gainsborough Old Hall, had been built by Sir Thomas Burgh and been used to entertain royalty, much as Scrooby Manor had been. Richard III stayed at the old Hall in 1484, as had Henry VIII with his last wife, Catherine Parr. It is still one of the finest medieval halls in England and open to the public. When the Burgh family fortunes declined in the 16th C, the hall was bought by the Hickmans, a family with strong Puritan sympathies.

Rose Hickman was a strong character. She escaped from England at the time of Bloody Mary and returned with her two children when Elizabeth came to the throne.

Gainsborough Old Hall, the home of the Hickman family

The Great Hall, Gainsborough Old Hall

Rose Hickman's son, William, became the owner and occupier of Gainsborough Old Hall. He had business interests in London and ran his properties on commercial lines. His Gainsborough tenants did not like him much, finding him less sympathetic to their problems than the easy-going Burghs had been.

Worshipping in Gainsborough

The Hickman family at the Old Hall were strong supporters of the Separatists and when the local Puritan ministers were kicked out of their churches for failing to follow the Prayer Book in their services, Rose Hickman invited one of them, Rev John Smyth, to hold services in her house so that they could worship in the way they wanted to. This was a very risky thing to do because they were holding an illegal service. If they had been caught, the worshippers would have been arrested and imprisoned. The Hickmans could have faced heavy fines and lost their home.

(by Lucy D. and Lauren B.)

Rose Hickman and her son, William, of Gainsborough Old Hall

For a time, both congregations continued undisturbed although it must have been difficult to avoid the notice of local busybodies who would be only too happy to report them to the authorities.

Early in 1607, Smyth and the Gainsborough church made good their escape and on reaching Amsterdam, began to worship with the earlier arrivals who called themselves the 'Ancient Brethren'. John Smyth was still restless in his faith. Having 'separated' from the Church of England, he now felt that the very basis of his faith was uncertain. He began to doubt that the English Bible was true to the original word of God and searched the Hebrew and Greek texts for deeper meaning.

For Smyth, and most of his followers, even their baptism seemed to be flawed. It had been carried out when they were infants without their agreement and within a flawed church. It was therefore doubly unsatisfactory. Smyth's radical solution was to baptise himself again, and then to baptise all the other members of his church. He became known as the Se-(or Self) Baptist. When Smyth died in Amsterdam in 1612, some of those who had followed him to Holland decided to return to England to form the first Baptist congregation in London.

5. Escape to Holland

In Scrooby, the small congregation meeting at the Manor began to plan their own escape from England. They were already in trouble for non-attendance at church and faced fines and imprisonment. They had no chance of getting official permission to leave for Holland, so they would have to go secretly. They began to sell their belongings to raise as much money as they could and planned their route to the coast. By the summer, those who had responsibilities quietly resigned from their jobs. William Brewster had given up his role as Postmaster by September 1607, and when the Archbishop's officers arrived in Scrooby to arrest him on suspicion of 'being a Brownist', he was nowhere to be found.   Their bird had flown.

The port of Boston had strong trading links with northern Europe and there were ships there which could take them across the North Sea. But Boston was sixty miles away across the Lincolnshire countryside. A large group of families travelling with their children and all their belongings would surely attract the suspicions of the authorities.

Map of England and Holland showing Scrooby (S), Boston (B) and
Immingham (I) in England, and Amsterdam (A), Leyden (L), Brill
(B) and Flushing (F) in Holland, by Thomas W.

One way to go was to travel south-east from Scrooby
down the old Roman road through Sturton le Steeple and
cross the River Trent at the ferry at Littleborough. The
Roman road went on through Sturton by Stow to the north
of Lincoln but they could skirt round Lincoln by
Skellingthorpe and walk across the heathland south of the

city to reach the backroads running down the valley of the River Witham to get to Boston.

High Bridge, Lincoln, the last bridge in England which still has houses built above the arches, as London Bridge had in Tudor times.

Another way would be to take a boat down the River Idle to the Trent, ride the flow tide up the river to Torksey and into the Fosse Dyke, the canal the Romans had built to link the River Trent to the Witham. If they went this way, they would pass right through Lincoln and under the High

Bridge in the heart of the city. If they were spotted and stopped, there would be nowhere to hide.

They decided to travel on foot, avoiding the towns, moving at night along quiet roads to reach the sea.

Betrayed

Their first attempt to leave England was in 1607, four hundred years ago this year. They walked all the way to Scotia Creek near Boston where they had secretly arranged for a ship to pick them up to take them across the North Sea to Holland. They were nervous but when night fell, they were relieved to get onto the ship, moored in the river Witham, not far from the sea.

But their captain had betrayed them. He had agreed to help them but was also working for the armed police. He kept his ship tied to the bank so that when the King's men came, the Scrooby group were abused and stripped of any valuables and then arrested. They had been caught breaking the law because they did not have permission to leave the country. They were all taken back to Boston where the leading men, including Brewster, were put in the cells in the Guildhall to await trial.

(by Maisie Y.)

Seven of the men, including Brewster, were kept in the Guildhall cells until the Boston Magistrates could meet in their courtroom above, and decide what to do with them. The Guildhall is still much the same today, with the cells still there and the stairs up to the court beside them. There was a delay which might have been because the town of Boston had strong Puritan sympathies but eventually the men were committed for trial at the next assizes at Lincoln.

Cells and stairs in Boston's Guildhall by Lucy G.

The women and children could not be tried as at that time they had no right to make their own decisions and hence could not be guilty of breaking the law. They were assumed to have followed their husbands' instructions. So they were allowed to find their way back to Scrooby. As they walked slowly home, Mary Brewster had her teenager son, Jonathan, to help her with seven year old Patience, and the baby, Fear. There was little at Scrooby to comfort them. They had already sold what they could not carry and had left their home at the Manor House. Now they had to find shelter in the modest cottages of friends in the village. There is no record of any prosecution against the seven men. Brewster and the others were eventually allowed to return home.

Trying again – the second attempt to escape

When their first attempt failed, they tried again in 1608. They had to pack up all their clothes and belongings and load them into boats at Scrooby. The women and children travelled as secretly as they could along the River Ryton to the River Idle. They had to go under Bawtry Bridge and on down the river to where it joins the Trent at West Stockwith. They must have been terrified of being caught when someone heard the tired children crying.

Going under Bawtry Bridge on the River Idle by Shannon L.

From the Trent, the current would take them down to the River Humber and they would sail out of the Humber to the open sea off the Lincolnshire coast. They planned to meet up with the men, who had travelled on foot overland, at a deserted place on the shore near Immingham but they got to the Humber too soon. Having to wait in the open sea, and feeling very sea-sick from the waves, they pleaded with the boatmen to go in to the shore. But when the tide went down, their boat got stuck in the mud. Meanwhile the captain of the

37

Dutch ship who had agreed to pick them all up, took the men on board first.

When the Dutch Captain saw a group of armed men coming along the shore, he did not want his ship to be caught, so he set sail. The women and children were left stranded on the shore devastated at what had happened.

(by Mollie C. and Chloe H.)

Left behind on the shore near Immingham by Molly I.

Sailing to Holland

The men were safe on the Dutch ship, but they had to watch what happened to the women and children they had been forced to leave behind on the shore. When they got out to sea, their ship encountered gales and high waves which covered the deck with water. For fourteen days, the passengers suffered terribly from sea-sickness, until, exhausted and miserable, they finally reached Holland. Eventually, the women and children left behind were *allowed to go as the authorities did not know what to do with them. As soon as they could, they joined the men in Holland.* *(by William B.)*

Dutch ship by Ryan R.

William Brewster already knew his way around Holland and probably spoke some Dutch. Twenty three years before he had come as an honoured guest with William Davison to help the Dutch to win back their country from the Spanish. They had been extraordinarily successful, driving back the Spanish army into the south of the Low Countries, in what is now Belgium. With freedom had come prosperity and a huge expansion of overseas trade. The merchants of Amsterdam set up the Dutch East India Company which controlled much of the valuable trade in spices from the Far East. Hard-working and practical, the Dutch had money to spend on fine houses and on works of art to decorate them. Frans Hals painted family portraits for the brewers of Haarlem while Rembrandt, born in the university city of Leyden, became rich and famous as an artist in Amsterdam.

The Scrooby women and children, accompanied by Brewster and some others of their menfolk, joined the men who had already settled in with the English living in Amsterdam. They did not stay for long. Distressed by the bitter arguments within Smyth's followers and the Ancient Brethren, they kept themselves apart as much as they could, while looking at the suitability of other Dutch cities as a more permanent home. To survive, they needed work, and most of them did not have a trade having been farmers back home in England.

It was John Robinson who wrote formally to the leaders of the city of Leyden, explaining that about a hundred English men and women wanted to join their community. King James of England got wind of this approach and tried to persuade the leaders of Leyden to reject the request but the City would not be bullied by the King of England. They had a long tradition of offering opportunities to newcomers and agreed to Robinson's request, provided that the English behaved well and followed the Dutch laws.

The Scrooby group had every intention of supporting themselves and avoiding trouble, and were assured by the City that they were welcome to settle in Leyden. When their preacher, Richard Clyfton, decided to stay in Amsterdam, the congregation elected William Brewster to be the Ruling Elder of their church. He was to be the assistant to John Robinson, their Preaching Elder and Pastor.

6. The Leyden church

The Scrooby group who moved to the university city of Leyden thought of themselves as a church, a group of Christians who wished to worship God in their own way. Leyden was a centre of the Dutch manufacture of textiles and there was work for those who had the right skills.. Weaving and carding wool, linen and cotton, dyeing the fibres and finishing the cloth were all trades controlled by the Dutch craft guilds and it was difficult for English-speaking, unskilled workers to make a living. Only by living simply in a close-knit community, and by working very hard, were they going to be able to survive in Leyden.

The New Rhine canal running through the heart of Leyden

Leyden is still the 'fair and beautiful city' that Bradford described. The River Rhine ran through the centre of the city and canals linked this to Amsterdam in the north. The Scrooby group landed by the city crane on May Day

1609, and found places to live. They clubbed together to buy a large house on the Kloksteel, or Bell Alley, which could be used for services and as a home for their pastor, John Robinson, Bridgit his wife and their family. It was near to St Peter's Church, and had a large garden, where they could build twenty one smaller cottages for the poorer members of their church. They could survive in Leyden by living simply, using the Tripe Market for cheap cuts of meat and by growing their own vegetables, but life must have been very hard.

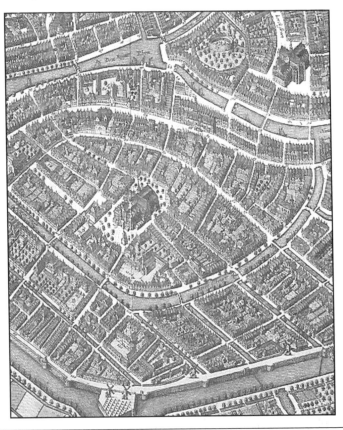

17th Century map of Leyden showing the canals, the two great churches of St Peter (centre) and St Pancras (top right), the round Castle keep and the city walls carrying windmills.

William and Mary Brewster lived nearby on a street called Sticksteeg, or Stink Alley, a name which did not seem to worry them. It now has a new name!

Leyden remembers William Brewster by naming the street in which he lived after him

Their fourth child, Love, was born there in 1611 and in 1614, their last son, Wrestling, was born. These strange names, together with Patience and Fear, are typical of a Puritan family. Parents expressed their need for 'patience in times of trouble', their 'fear of the Lord', the 'love of God' for them as a family and their 'wrestling for the truth' about God, in the names of their children, a daily reminder of the faith that was central to every aspect of their lives.

For a time, William Bradford lived with them but, when he was 21 in 1611, he inherited some money, bought his own house and got married to Dorothy, the daughter of one of the Ancient Brethren in Amsterdam. There were many marriages within the Leyden church including the Brewster's eldest son, Jonathan, in 1615, but there were also many deaths in the English families, especially of children. Outside St Peter's Church, (the Pieterskerk today), there is a list of over thirty family members who died in the years that they were in the city. For a time, Jonathan Brewster worked as a ribbon maker in Leyden while his father made good use of his English and Latin, and his smattering of Dutch, by giving lessons to the young Dutch students who attended the University.

The family had enough money to survive but they were not rich. There was space in their house for a small business venture and it had a side entrance onto another alley, called Choir Alley. William went into partnership with an Englishman he trusted, Thomas Brewer, who had money to invest. Together they set up a small printing press in the Brewster's top floor. The Choir Alley Press started to publish books in Dutch, English and Latin, but only the first three actually carried his name.

Printing books in Leyden

When the Scrooby group reached Leyden, they were free to worship God in the way they wanted to, but they had to support themselves. William Brewster worked as a printer, making books in his house. Some of these were about King James, and criticised his leadership of the Church in England. Because they were printed in Holland, Brewster arranged for them to be smuggled into England. When King James heard about this, he asked the Dutch to find Brewster's press and shut it down.

(by Jordan F.)

One of the books which were printed anonymously in English and particularly angered King James was called 'The Perth Assembly'. It was written by a Scottish religious leader to resist James' attempt to force the church in Scotland to accept the English Prayer Book. The King and Bishops had called the Assembly to tell the Scottish leaders that they would have to follow English Church rules which the Scots resented deeply, particularly having to accept the authority of Bishops.

The author's rejection of all these regulations was written in a style guaranteed to provoke the King's anger. The King's officers suspected that the book had been printed in Holland and secretly taken back to Scotland for distribution amongst church leaders. Most of these fully agreed with the objections the book raised but it was dangerous to be so outspoken. As the book had no printer's name in it, when copies were seized by the King's men, the print was checked for other clues. Sometimes small faults in the letter-type which a printer used showed which press had produced it and this may have led the English authorities to Brewster. The English Ambassador in Holland found a copy and tried to persuade the Dutch authorities to close down the press.

Printed Anno Dom. 1617.

The bookplate showing a bear which some believe Brewster used in the books that he printed in Choir Alley, Leyden

Even under pressure from the King, the Dutch refused to shut down the Press, but there was another way. At first, in Holland, printing was not controlled as it was in England. But the Dutch later decided to bring in a system of licensing for books. Even if Brewster had not printed the most offensive book, many of those he had printed had been done without a licence from the Dutch States General. They raided his house and confiscated his type, press and remaining books. The Choir Alley Press was closed for good. But before he could be arrested, William Brewster disappeared. Neither the Dutch authorities nor King James' agents could find him

There were other reasons why the members of the Leyden church were becoming increasingly restless. After over ten years of living in Holland, they felt that they had not yet found a permanent home. The peace between Holland and Spain was very fragile and could break down at any time, returning the country to a savage war. The Leyden church knew of the suffering of the city during the last terrible seige by the Spanish Army. The Dutch had liberated their city but only by breaking the dykes and letting the sea flood the surrounding farm-land. It had taken years for the area to recover.

Religious disagreements were also tearing the Dutch churches apart. In the old traditions of the Roman Catholic church, men had been offered the chance to earn their way to heaven by doing penances or even buying what were called 'indulgences'. These, the church taught, built up your credit with God and could earn access to heaven. This meant that those who could afford to buy indulgences had an unfair advantage. In Germany, Martin Luther had challenged this system, provoking what is now called the Reformation and the start of the Protestant churches.

Luther taught that God offers everyone the opportunity to believe in Jesus Christ so that they can be saved and go to heaven. They did not have to pay a price because Christ has already paid by his death on the Cross and the story of that is told in the gospels, or Good News, of the Bible. But since the time of John Calvin of Geneva, many of the reformed churches had followed his teaching that God himself chooses who will be saved and who will be damned.

John Calvin of Geneva, 1509-1564

This idea of pre-destination seems to leave men powerless. Only those who are predestined to be saved will respond to the preaching of the Gospel. At the University of Leyden, Jacob Arminius began to teach that Calvin was wrong and God could give men a choice, either to accept faith in God or to reject it. This new teaching is now widely accepted in the Christian church, but at the time, it caused great conflict, especially in Holland, just at the time the group from Scrooby were beginning to wonder whether they should stay in Leyden. They had always believed that God had chosen them to be His followers. Now perhaps they had a choice. As the argument in Leyden grew into a great split in the Dutch church, which even led to war, the small group of English believers became more and more sure that it was time to leave again, before their children forgot their faith.

Letter to Rose Hickman, of the Old Hall, Gainsborough
Stink Alley, Leyden, Holland.   *Easter 1617*

My loving and much beloved Lady Rose

    We remember your great kindness in welcoming us to Gainsborough. God has been good to us in our new home in Leyden, but after ten years living here, my husband and I, along with the other parents in our church, are increasingly worried about our children. They seem to have forgotten why we came here and are turning into Dutch children, changing their language and going to parties. The idea of coming here originally was to be able to practise our religion freely, something which our children seem to have forgotten. William and I have prayed about this and have decided that it is time for us to leave. We must sell everything we can to raise money to start a new life somewhere else, where our children will not face the same temptations.

    Your grateful friend,   Dorothy Brewster

    (By Elisha T. and Zoe A.)

Brewster, Robinson and the other leaders discussed where they should go to make a fresh start. They considered moving to Virginia, where the English had already established a settlement at Jamestown. They even considered Guiana in South America where Sir Walter Raleigh had tried to set up a colony but thought that it would be too hot and unhealthy. The New World on the other side of the Atlantic seemed very tempting but very far away.

Journey to Unknown lands

Ever since the Spanish discovered the New World and set up colonies there, America had a dazzling reputation as a land of riches and opportunity. Men from all the other European nations dreamt of getting to this wonderful place. They took no account of the dangers which lurked in these unknown lands, including the people who were already there, the American Indians, who might not welcome them at all.

(by Elizabeth G.)

The Leyden church bought a copy of Captain John Smith's Map of New England and studied it with great interest. He had advised would-be settlers that this most northerly area of what the English called Virginia was a land of opportunity, not as a source of gold but as a place where a *'man may be master and owner of his own labour and land. If he have nothing but his hands, he may set up his trade and by industry quickly grow rich.'*

To go to any part of Virginia meant getting permission from King James. This would not be easy as most of them had left England without permission and with charges to face if they ever returned. They decided to send representatives back to England to try to negotiate with the Virginia Company.

Brewster also knew an individual who could help them. As Steward to the Archbishop of York at Scrooby, he and his father before him had served Archbishop Sandys whose son, Sir Edwin Sandys, was now an influential man in London. He was also sympathetic to the Puritans, as his father had been. From the start of the London Virginia Company, Sandys had been an investor and leading member of the Company Council. He had been responsible for drafting the first Royal Charter and, by the time the Leyden church needed his help, he was in a position to be useful to them.

Robinson and Brewster sent a letter to the Council of the London Virginia Company carried by two representatives of their church, the two Deacons, John Carver and Robert Cushman. Strictly speaking, the London Company could only give approval for a settlement as far north as Manhattan Island but this might be far enough. Although the area which John Smith's map called New England was further north, there was plenty of space between Jamestown and Manhattan.

Carver and Cushman got an encouraging response from Sandys and the Council of the Virginia Company who were keen to recruit more colonists for Virginia, but there was a problem, the matter of religion. If the Leyden church could agree to become loyal members of the Church of England, or the King's Church' as they called it, it would be relatively easy to get permission to settle in Virginia. But the Leyden church would not compromise on matters of religion. They had escaped from the 'King's Church' and had no wish to go back. If they admitted to being 'Separatists' or even worse were thought to be 'Brownists', the King and his advisers were hardly likely to approve their settlement in an area which was still directly under the King's authority. So Brewster and Robinson sent a series of carefully worded letters to Sandys and the Council. They first set out 'seven principles' for their plan, accepting the King's authority, but 'only if the thing commanded be not against God's word'. The idea that every Royal requirement would be tested against the Bible by a group of independent church members suspected of printing seditious literature, was clearly not acceptable in London!

Sandys tried again. 'Could they reconsider their position as the Council were still thinking about it?' Robinson and Brewster scratched their heads and took up their pens. This time they reduced their comments to five principles, that they trusted God to 'graciously prosper our endeavours', that they had already survived in a 'strange and hard land' and 'were weaned from the delicate milk of our mother country', that their group were as 'industrious and frugal as any company of people in the world', that their 'strict and sacred bond and covenant' would help them to look after each other.

Lastly, they explained, they were burning their boats in leaving Holland for America and would not expect either to return or to be looked after. In short, if the Council would support their venture, they would commit themselves to make a success of their settlement and 'be no further troublesome' to the Council or to the King. There was no mention of their wish to practice their religion without interference.

Their good reputation with the Dutch, who both admired their hard work and respected their honesty, helped them. Members of the Council spoke up for them when the matter was considered by the King and emphasised that they would try to both spread the Gospel and extend English influence in the New World. When he asked how they proposed to support themselves, an inspired response 'by fishing', won King James' approval. 'Fishing' said the King, 'so God have my soul, 'tis an honest trade. 'Twas the Apostles' own calling.'

Carver and Cushman kept up the exchange of letters as the two sides inched towards an agreement. Robinson and Brewster knew that they would never get the full approval of the English Church authorities while they were known to follow church practices in Leyden which were still illegal in England. They claimed that the way their church functioned was close to the practices of the 'French Reformed Church,' knowing that most members of the Church of England would have little idea just what these were and assume that they were similar to their own.

Eventually, Robinson and Brewster agreed to appear to accept much of what the King and the Bishops demanded, without actually saying so. By the time they were 3,000 miles away on the other side of the Atlantic, they would be free to follow their own consciences without much interference from England. As Bradford put it, *'they presumed they should not be troubled'*. Wisely keeping Brewster's name out of their submission, they were granted a 'patent' to settle in Virginia, dated June 9th 1619 in the name of John Wincop, who worked for Elizabeth Clinton Fynnes, the Countess of Lincoln. The way to America seemed to be clear.

As they always did when considering an important decision, the Leyden church came together for a *'solemn meeting and day of humiliation'* led by Pastor Robinson with sermons and prayers. They decided to go, in spite of all the difficulties. But they also decided to divide into two groups. Some would remain in Leyden with their Pastor and ordained Minister, John Robinson. About half of the church would leave with their Ruling Elder, William Brewster, and sail to Virginia. They all knew each other well so those who stayed would look after some of the children of those who went. At some later date, Robinson and those remaining in Leyden would join the others in the New World.

Letter to our friends in Boston, England

Leyden, Holland   *July 1620*

Dear Mary

I hope that you are all well in Boston. Thank you for visiting us when we in the cells in the Guild Hall. Eventually we managed to get out of England and go to Holland. My Mum and Dad now think we should move on, to a new life in New England. I don't want to go because I may never see my friends again. We plan to leave sometime soon.

Please write a letter to me in America.

From your loving friend
             Sophie W.

The group leaving for America would have no ordained minister until Robinson could join them, as Brewster had never been ordained. For however long it took, he would be solely responsible for preaching, teaching and leading their acts of worship. Without Robinson, they would not be able to celebrate the sacrament of Communion.

There were other more practical matters to attend to. They soon realised that their finances would not cover the full cost of such a venture. They might be able to afford the purchase of a small ship and enough supplies for their group of about forty to survive for a time, but their chances of making their setttlement permanent would be much greater if they had more people and more money. They got in touch with Thomas Weston, a London Merchant Adventurer who was already active in trading, legal and illegal, with Holland. He came to Leyden and made them an offer. Rather than going under the auspices of the Virginia Company, Weston would find backers for them from rich investors, or Adventurers, in London.

They would invest in the new colony as a joint stock company, just as the investors in the Jamestown venture had done. Early profits would not come from finding gold but from the rich fishing and fur-trading which was already bringing a return to wise investors in American ventures, or so he promised them. They would get a patent from the Virginia Company by applying as Adventurers making no mention of the Pilgrims and their religious commitment.

The Leyden church agreed to join forces with Weston's 'Adventurers' because they thought the terms were reasonable. Weston promptly changed these to their disadvantage. They would have to work more days per week for the company, up from five to seven, and have to wait seven years before they would have their own land. Carver and Cushman, as the Leyden church representatives, reluctantly agreed. When this became known in Leyden, the church members protested. They thought that the new arrangement were '*more fit for thieves and bond-slaves than honest men*' and some withdrew. But the majority were already so heavily committed to leaving Holland that they had little choice. The arrangements descended further into chaos when another agent claiming to be acting for them started to buy up provisions for the voyage without consulting Carver. It was not a good start for such a risky venture.

7. Becoming Pilgrims

They had started from Scrooby and became known as the Scrooby Separatists. They spent nearly twelve years in Leyden and became the Leyden church. Writing much later, William Bradford gave them the new name by which they are known today, in his account of their departure from Holland. '*They knew they were pilgrims, and looked not much on those things, but lifted up their eyes to the heavens, their dearest country, and quietened their spirits.*' But first they had to get to England to link up with the Adventurers. Just where William Brewster was at this time is something of a mystery. He was still in hiding, either in Leiderdorp just outside Leyden, or somewhere in England.

Not able to afford the best of ships, they bought the *Speedwell*, a small pinnace which could carry sixty tons which they planned to keep in the New World as the basis of their fishing project. None of them knew anything about ships or fishing and the suspicion is that the *Speedwell's* Captain never intended to sail the Atlantic in her. He replaced her masts at their expense, a change which was to prove disastrous when she met the heavy winds of the Channel, let alone the open ocean.

They also decided to recruit a soldier whom Robinson trusted, Miles Standish, to be responsible for their defences when they reached Virginia. They were under no illusions that the American Indians would receive them in peace and Standish was an experienced veteran of the campaigns against the Spanish. Another even more experienced soldier and explorer, Captain John Smith of Jamestown, had offered his services as well as selling them his map, but they turned him down. He was not the easiest of men to fit into a community of deeply religious families and he was probably too expensive anyway.

The group who were leaving distributed the things they did not think they would need amongst their friends in Leyden. Those of their families who were staying in Leyden found new homes. Mary Brewster decided to take ten year old, Love, and their youngest, six year old, Wrestling, with them but left Jonathan to continue to work in Leyden. Patience and Fear stayed too, with the Robinson family. As William had requested, Mary also packed all the books in William's library to take with them, no doubt grumbling as wives do about their husbands' priorities. William and Mary Bradford left their only son, John, then just six years old, with friends.

In July 1620, after a service and supper, the whole church, and even some of their friends from Amsterdam, helped those who were going to load their belongings into a canal boat on the Rhine running through Leyden. Together, they set off south, passing through the city of Delft to the point where the Rhine canal joined the estuary of the Maas, at Delftshaven, where the *Speedwell* was waiting for them.

This is now in the west of modern Rotterdam in the one part of the city that was not flattened by bombing in the Second World War. The canal still has old Dutch sailing barges moored to the banks and the church where John Robinson preached a farewell sermon still stands by the water's edge.

Delftshaven, where John Robinson said farewell to the Pilgrims leaving on the Speedwell to sail to England.

With John Robinson's farewell prayer ringing in their ears, they went aboard, *'the tide, which stays for no man, calling them away'*. A *'prosperous wind'* took them swiftly across the Channel to Southampton, where Carver, Cushman, Weston and the Adventurers were waiting for them in the larger ship, the *Mayflower*. William Brewster came out of hiding and slipped on board.

At Southampton, the arguments continued, with Weston demanding that the Pilgrims agree to the new terms. When they refused, Weston withdrew all further financial help and the Pilgrims had to sell some of their supplies to pay for the work that had been done on the *Speedwell* . As they had more butter than they needed, thanks to the confusion over who was supposed to be buying what, this was not too much of a hardship. On August 5th, they sailed at last, the *Speedwell* carrying most of the Pilgrims and the *Mayflower* with the Adventurers. Just before they left, a letter from John Robinson was read, encouraging them to establish a proper system of government, so they chose Christopher Martin to lead those on the *Mayflower* and their Deacon, Robert Cushman, those on the *Speedwell*.

Mayflower II, the full scale replica ship now moored at Plymouth, Massachusetts

Out in the Channel, the *Speedwell* soon began to leak. Her new masts put too much strain on the hull and they had to put in to the port of Dartmouth for more repairs, and yet more expense. When they tried again, even before they reached Landsend, the leaking *Speedwell* began to fill up. Hastily returning to the safety of Plymouth, they were faced with a decision. Although the *Mayflower* was really only large enough to take the Adventurers, they could not go without the Pilgrims. Some of the Adventurers gave up the idea of going to Virginia and left. Transferring their belongings to the hold of the larger ship, the Pigrim families joined the Adventurers in the already crowded space on the *Mayflower's* gun deck. There were now seventy men and women and thirty-two children in a space about seventy feet long and twelve feet wide.

Family spaces for passengers on the replica Mayflower's gun deck

At last they were ready to leave Plymouth, on September 6th 1620. The first few days of their voyage were calm and peaceful and the two groups, most of whom had never met each other before could get to know each other. They were very different. The Pilgrims had been living and worshipping together for years and shared a conviction that the God who had brought them out of England would ensure that they reached their 'promised land' of America. Their fellow passengers were a mixed bag of English men and women, with no more than the general interest in religion that all in the seventeenth century had. Some hoped to make their fortunes in America, some were hired hands brought along as servants.

Storm at sea

When we first set sail from England, the weather was bright and sunny. But the wind got stronger and soon we were in a terrible storm. On the Mayflower, it was really rough and one of the boys was blown overboard, only to be saved by a trailing rope. The wind blew so hard that the ship rocked from side to side. People were being sea-sick over the side of the ship. Some of us didn't make it to the side and were sick in their beds. The smell was revolting. There were no toilets on our ship, so we had to hang over the bows and watch out for big waves!

(by Lauren S.)

Captain Christopher Jones' crew were as tough a bunch of seamen as you would find on any ship. They had no sympathy for the soft passengers unused to such rough conditions and openly mocked them. One of the younger seamen was particularly abusive and told them all that they would die at sea and find a watery grave. When he was the first to become ill and died '*in a desperate manner and so was the first that was thrown overboard*', the Pilgrims believed that his profanity had been punished by God Himself.

Voyage to America

In the sixty five days it took the Mayflower to reach the North American coast, only one of the passengers died of disease. But the ship was blown off course and in the middle of the ocean, a big storm hit the ship. They were terrified that the Mayflower would sink and they would all drown. Somehow, they managed to stop the ship from breaking up and eventually the storm eased. They had been blown far to the north. When they eventually reached the American coast, they realised that they were not in Virginia as they had planned, but much further north.

(by Heather P.)

At the height of the storm, the great beam that held the ship together *'was bowed and cracked which put them in some fear'*. The Pilgrims offered the Captain the use of a *'great screw'* to jack up the beam and hold it in place for the rest of the voyage. Perhaps this was from the Brewster press.

They had planned to settle in the extreme north of the Virginia Company's territory, in what is now the Manhattan region around New York, but in November 1620, the Pilgrims recognised their first sight of land. It was the strange curved spit which was shown on John Smith's map as Cape James, but which sailors knew as Cape Cod. For a time, they tried to sail south, but found that the shoals along the coast were so dangerous that Christopher Jones took his ship round the head of the Cape and into the calm waters of a safe harbour. They moored in what is still called Cape Cod Bay, near to the point where Provincetown now lies.

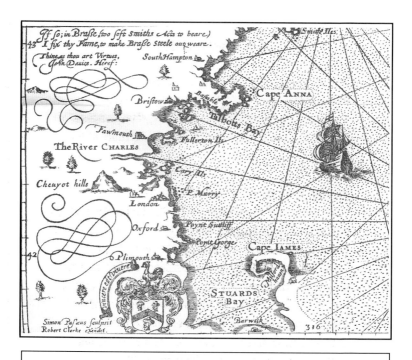

Southern New England on John Smith's map showing 'Plymouth' on the west side of 'Stuards Bay' (Cape Cod Bay), 'Cape James' (Cape Cod), and the 'River Charles' which is still called that, to the north of what is now the city of Boston, Massachusetts.

They had arrived in their 'promised land' or rather the Pilgrims in the party had arrived. For the Adventurers, landfall did not have quite the same significance but if they were to survive, they realised that they would have to work together. Brewster and Bradford drew up a document for all the men to sign. It has become known as the Mayflower Compact, and was to provide the principles on which they would set up the *'civil body politic'*, their new community.

The Mayflower Compact

In the name of God, Amen. We, whose names are underwritten, the Loyal Subjects of our dread Sovereign Lord, King James, by the Grace of God, of England, France and Ireland, King, Defender of the Faith, e&.

Having undertaken for the Glory of God, and Advancement of the Christian Faith, and the Honour of our King and Country, a voyage to plant the first colony in the northern parts of Virginia; do by these presents, solemnly and mutually in the Presence of God and one of another, covenant and combine ourselves together into a civil Body Politick, for our better Ordering and Preservation, and Furtherance of the Ends aforesaid; And by Virtue hereof to enact, constitute, and frame, such just and equal Laws, Ordinances, Acts, Constitutions and Offices, from time to time, as shall be thought most meet and convenient for the General good of the Colony; unto which we promise all due submission and obedience.

In Witness whereof we have hereunto subscribed our names at Cape Cod the eleventh of November, in the Reign of our Sovereign Lord, King James of England, France and Ireland, the eighteenth, and of Scotland the fifty-fourth. Anno Domini, 1620.

(There followed the forty one signatures of the men amongst the Pilgrims and Adventurers on the Mayflower, at anchor in Providence Bay, Cape Cod.)

They chose one of the Pilgrims, John Carver, to be their first Governor and planned to explore their new surroundings around Cape Cod Bay. Stored in sections on the Mayflower was a 'shallop', an open boat in which they could row or sail from the ship into the shallow waters along the shore. Assembling the boat and making her watertight took time and energy but they were soon ready. They found a sandy shore with shallow rivers running into the sea, not unlike the coast of Lincolnshire they had first left and the Dutch coast west of Leyden.

On the shores of Cape Cod Bay, Massachusetts

8. Plymouth Plantation

In early December, while William Bradford was away exploring the coast, his young wife Mary fell overboard from the Mayflower and was drowned in the cold water of the Bay. It must have been a devastating blow to the young man who was become such a pillar of the new community.

On John Smith's map, the Pilgrims knew of the place-name 'Plymouth', put there on a whim by Charles, Prince of Wales in 1616. When the Pilgrims explored the west side of Cape Cod Bay, they found a good anchorage which they named Plymouth Bay and an area of open ground with a clear stream giving a good source of water. They used a large rock to step ashore from their boat. It has become a point of pilgrimage for countless Americans.

The Plymouth Rock Memorial, Plymouth, Massachusetts.

Arriving in the New World

Those who were fit enough when they reached Plymouth started to put up shelters near to the beach and then searched for good land on which they could grow their food.

Had it not been for friendly American Indians, the Pilgrims would not have survived. They taught them the skills of hunting and trapping, woodcraft and how to make maple syrup to sweeten their food, moccasins for their feet and birch-bark canoes to travel in. They learnt how to grow crops like sweetcorn and beans. The Indians also showed the Pilgrims how to catch the wild turkeys which lived in the woods.

(by Elizabeth G. and Heather P.)

As it was, many more of the Pilgrims did not survive that first winter in New England. Weakened by the long voyage and struggling to keep warm in the bitter cold, one by one they fell ill and died. One new baby had been born on the voyage, aptly christened 'Oceanus', but many of the children died. The handful of Pilgrims who remained fit enough to work, struggled to fell trees and build a simple meeting house to shelter the sick and to use for worship on Sundays.

William Brewster, although he was at fifty-three one of the oldest, kept working and encouraging the others. They started to build small timber cottages for each family. *'Plymouth Colony'* began to put down roots. By the time the Spring came in March 1621, forty-three of the *Mayflower's* passengers had died but the survivors had a foothold on the American shore. In April, the *Mayflower* sailed back to England and they were on their own. Not quite alone though, thanks to the friendly American Indians.

Two of these were particularly helpful. One day just before the *Mayflower* left, a tall Indian walked into the Plymouth settlement and spoke to them in 'broken English'. His name was Samoset. A few days later, he brought more Indians with him and the tools that had been stolen from

Plymouth. He announced that the local chief would also visit. His name was Massasoit and he came with an entourage of his people including an Indian called Squanto. Squanto's English was better than Somoset's and his story was even more extraordinary.

Many years before, an English ship had sailed into the Bay and taken him with other Indians back to England. He became a servant in the household of Sir Ferdinando Gorges in Plymouth and learned to speak English. When Captain John Smith visited Gorges and planned his voyage to New England in 1614, he took Squanto with him, intending to leave him in the area of his old home. But the Captain who sailed with Smith used Squanto to help him to capture more members of his people who were all taken to Spain and sold as slaves.

Eventually, Squanto escaped and found a ship sailing to Newfoundland. Once there, one of Gorges' old captains recognised him as 'Sir Ferdinando's Indian'. He took Squanto back to England where, yet again, Gorges sent him back to the New England coast. When Squanto finally did return to his home, he found that his people had been wiped out by smallpox introduced by contact with European sailors. For two years, Squanto helped the Pilgrims. When he fell ill and lay dying in 1622, he asked the Governor, William Bradford, to pray for him so *"he could go to the white man's heaven"*. The Pilgrims called him *'a special instrument sent of God for their good'*.

Massasoit, the chief of the Wapanoag people living around Plymouth, agreed a peace treaty with the settlement which provided for *'no injury or hurt'* from one side against the other, for the handing over of any offenders, a mutual defence agreement against common enemies and an agreement that both sides should approach the other unarmed. For a time, the two peoples lived side by side, and in the autumn of 1621, when the Pilgrims had gathered in their first harvest in the New World, they invited the Indians to join them in a great Thanksgiving Feast.

'Our Harvest being gotten in, our governor sent four men on fowling, that we might after a special manner rejoice together after we had gathered up the fruit of our labors. The four, in one day, killed as much fowl as ...served the company almost a week. At which time...many of the Indians coming amongst us...and their greatest king Massasoit, with some ninety men, whome for three days we entertained and feasted, and killed five deer which they brought to the plantation and bestowed on our governor. And although it be not always so plentiful as it was at this time with us, yet by the goodness of God, we were so far from want.....' (Edward Winslow, writing to a friend in England, 1621.)

This first Thanksgiving, has became the model for all such celebrations in the United States ever since, although President Abraham Lincoln moved the date of the national holiday to the fourth Thursday in November. For the Pilgrims, plentiful deer and turkey in the woods, their own harvest of Indian corn, the shelter of their newly built homes and peace with the Indians meant that they could look forward to survival through the coming winter. They stayed in peace with Massasoit's people, although Captain Standish carried out a pre-emptive attack on the neighbouring people, the Massachusetts, who had offended and threatened him. A number were killed in the raid and their heads brought back to Plymouth. When news of this reached John Robinson still in Leyden, he wrote that he disapproved of such killings, advising them to be more concerned to convert the Indians than to kill them.

American Indian house and corn field at Plymouth Plantation

In 1621 and again in 1623, ships from Europe brought family members to Plymouth from Leyden and England, including Jonathan Brewster and his two sisters, Patience and Fear, now grown women.

Governor Bradford welcomed Alice Southworth, a young widow with two children who had stayed in Leyden and came on the second ship. They were married a few days after her arrival. By the end of 1623, almost all of those the Pilgrims had left behind in Leyden had joined them at Plymouth Plantation.

Ship from England by Sophie T.

But none of the ships brought the man they most hoped to see, John Robinson. The Adventurers had strongly opposed him joining the Plymouth colony and now it seemed that he would never come. Instead, a minister called Lydford was sent out by the Adventurers but he turned out to be a thoroughly bad lot and was eventually forced to leave the colony.

In 1625, the Plymouth community heard that their beloved Pastor had died in Leyden. John Robinson was buried in the church just near his house, the Pieterskerk, where his memorial can still be seen. William Brewster continued to serve as the spiritual leader of the Plymouth community. For twenty four years, he preached and taught in the meeting house that became their church.

Homes and gardens in the reconstructed 'Plymouth Plantation'

For Mary Brewster who had endured so much alongside the other women in the early days of the settlement, the arrival of her son and daughters must have been a joyous time. Life was still hard, and a far cry from the life she and William had shared in the comfort and space of Scrooby Manor House, but at least they were alive and together. They had fish and lobster from the sea and venison from the woods. They kept chickens, pigs and goats in their yard, and grew vegetables in their small gardens together with herbs to treat the sickness that all had to accept as part of life without modern medicine.

For a time, all the Brewster children lived with or near William and Mary in their house at Plymouth. Their eldest son, Jonathan, married again and the first of his eight children was soon toddling around to visit his grandmother. Patience married later that same year when her husband arrived on the *Fortune*. They had five children before Patience died. Her husband remarried and had four more.

Inside a house at 'Plymouth Plantation' today, with large radish!

Fear Brewster, who came with her parents on the *Mayflower*, married another passenger twice her age whose own wife had died in the first winter. He already had three children and together they had a son. Mary's youngest boys, Fear and Wrestling, lived with them in the simple timber cottage within the settlement, close to the Bradfords' house. We know little about Wrestling except that he is said to have *'died young without marrying'*.

Mary was not well for most of the time she had at Plymouth and in 1627 she died. William, as Elder of the church, led her funeral service and buried her alongside the graves of all the others who had died.

By then the colony had become a small township. A central roadway ran down from the meeting house, which also served as a fort, between two rows of houses to the gate out through the surrounding palisade. The replica township now called '*Plymouth Plantation*' depicts this well, complete with interpreters in period costume and accurate stories to tell visitors.

Love Brewster married Sarah Collier in 1634. She was the daughter of one of the Adventurers and by the time of the wedding, the two groups, Pilgrims and Adventurers, had long been integrated into one community. In the same year, William Brewster moved from Plymouth to a new settlement to the north in an area called Duxborrow where the land was better for farming. He and Captain Standish both bought land on what became known as 'The Captain's Nook' jutting out into Plymouth Bay. The area is now included in the Myles Standish State Reservation just to the south of modern South Duxbury.

Although he was still responsible as Elder for the Plymouth Church, Brewster was also made Elder of the new church at Duxburrow. The farming community prospered and grew under the wise leadership of Governor William Bradford. Brewster had collected a large library of books, adding to those he brought with him on the *Mayflower*. There were many religious books in Latin alongside more practical volumes of advice on medicine and farming. Some he had signed, so we know how he wrote his name.

But of the man himself, there is no image, just a wealth of imaginative portraits which now hang in important places in the United States of America.

One of the Gainsborough Parish School team, after thinking about what Brewster must have been like by the time he sat in the sun looking out over his farm at Duxburrow, produced her own portrait of William Brewster in old age, a wise and gentle man with the strength of a prophet and the sense of purpose of a pilgrim..

William Brewster in old age by Danielle M.

His friend William Bradford described his character in this glowing tribute.

'For his personal abilities, he was qualified above many; he was wise and discreet and well spoken, having a grave and deliberate utterance, of a very cheerful spirit, very sociable and pleasant amongst his friends, of an humble and modest mind, of a peaceable disposition, undervaluing himself and his own abilities, inoffensive and innocent in his life and conversation. He was tender-hearted, and compassionate of such as were in misery, but especially of such as had been of good estate and rank, and were fallen into want and poverty, either for goodness and religion's sake, or by the injury and oppression of others.'
(from Bradford's 'Life and Death of Elder Brewster', 1643)

In 1643 the Civil War between Parliament and King Charles was tearing England apart. Three thousand miles to the west, in the Plymouth Colony, the man who had led his little flock out of England to avoid submitting to the authority of the King's father, reached the end of his long life. At the last, William Brewster died a good death, as he had lived a good life.

'About the 18th of April died their Reverend Elder and my dear and loving friend Mr William Brewster, a man that had done and suffered much for the Lord Jesus and the gospel's sake, and had borne his part in weal and woe with this poor persecuted church above 36 years in England, Holland and in this wilderness, and done the Lord and them faithful service in his place and calling. And notwithstanding the many troubles and sorrows he passed through, the Lord upheld him to a great age. He was near fourscore years of age when he died. He had this blessing added by the Lord to all the rest; to die in his bed, in peace, amongst the midst of his friends...'
(William Bradford 1643)

Postscript

This short account of the life of William Brewster is the sixth book to be written and illustrated with the help of pupils from schools in Eastern England as part of the ARIES (American Roots in English Soil) Project.

Jamestown was first settled in 1607 and to mark the 400th anniversary of Jamestown a series of books has been published: 'Captain John Smith and the Founding of America'; 'Mrs John Rolfe – better known as Pocahontas'; 'Admiral of New England – Captain John Smith and the American Dream' 'Captain Christopher Newport of Limehouse, Jamestown and the East Indies'; 'Captain Bartholomex Gosnold of Otley and America' (to be published in May 2007)

Thirteen years after Jamestown was first established, the Pilgrim Fathers landed at Plymouth near Cape Cod and established their settlement. Ten years after that, the Massachusetts Bay Company settled the area to the north of Plymouth and founded the large colony which grew into the City of Boston, Massachusetts. Lastly, the Catholics established their first settlements in Maryland. All these developments in early American history have their roots in the rich soil of Eastern England.

This account of the life of William Brewster is the first of the 'New England' series of titles, which will also include titles on Anne Hutchinson, Simon and Anne Bradstreet, John Cotton and the Boston Men, and the Calverts of Maryland. We hope that you enjoy reading them as much as we have enjoyed writing, illustrating and publishing them.

William Brewster: An outline chronology

1492	Columbus 'discovers' the New World
1564	William Shakespeare born
1567	William Brewster thought to have been born, possibly in Scrooby, but no record exists
1580	William Brewster goes to Cambridge University
1583	Joins Davison as Secretary
1588	Defeat of the Spanish Armada
1589	Returns to Scrooby, father dies in 1590; Brewster takes over as Queen's Postmaster and Steward to Archbishop of York
1591	Brewster marries Mary; they have six children: Jonathan, Patience, Fear, Love, Wrestling, and one who died as a baby
1591-1604	still at Scrooby, Brewster meets with William Bradford and starts to worship away from the Parish Church, first at Babworth (Richard Clyfton), then at Gainsborough (John Smyth)
1603	Elizabeth 1 dies; James VI of Scotland becomes James I of England and Scotland
1604	Hampton Court conference; James meets with bishops and puritan clergy to decide church issues; King James Bible commissioned to replace Geneva Bible but Puritans failed to persuade King to reform church; they are told 'conform' or be 'harried out of the land'.
1605	Gunpowder plot fails
1606	Gainsborough group split; Brewster starts Separatist worship in Scrooby Manor; Smyth takes his group to Holland
1606	December: Virginia Company fleet sails to settle Jamestown (May 1607); Brewster goes

	into hiding and plans to escape with Scrooby group from Boston
1607	Arrested and imprisoned at Boston, Lincs.
1608	Second attempt to escape succeeds from Immingham; Brewsters reach Holland
1609	Separatists move to Leyden; Brewster starts printing business in Leyden, gets into trouble because of books attacking James I
1619	Separatists get permission to move to 'Virginia'; buy the Speedwell and sail for England;
1620	Link up with others and sail for America on the Mayflower; 11.11.1620: Mayflower Compact signed; land at Plymouth, Massachusetts
1621	11.12.1621; first Thanksgiving; Treaty signed with American Indians
1623	Dutch settle New Amsterdam which later becomes New York
1625	Charles I becomes king; plague in London
1627	Mary Brewster dies at Plymouth, Massachusetts;
1630	Massachusetts Bay Company establishes new settlement at Boston, Massachusetts
1631	Captain John Smith dies in London
1633/4	epidemic of the Plague at Plymouth, Mass; Patience and Fear die;Brewster moves from Plymouth to Duxbury farm 10 miles north; Brewster remains as Elder of Plymouth church and also elder of Duxbury church
1643	William Brewster dies in April 'in his bed, in peace, amongst the midst of his friends'; he was almost 80.
1649	Charles I executed

Sources

We used the following sources to research this book

Adair, John
> '*Founding Fathers, the Puritans in England and North America*', J M Dent and Sons, 1982

Arber, Edward Ed.
> '*Travels and Works of Captain John Smith*' 2nd Ed. A.G Bradley Edinburgh 1910

Beale, David,
> '*The Mayflower Pilgrims: roots of Puritan, Presbyterian and Baptist Heritage*', Ambassador-Emerald International, *2000*

Bradford, William.
> '*Of Plymouth Plantation, 1620-1647*' Edited by Samuel E Morison, Alfred A Knopf, New York 2001

Cheetham, Keith,
> '*On the Trail of the Pilgrim Fathers*', pb 2001

Deetz, J and P S,
> '*The Times of their Lives*' W H Freeman, New York 2000

Sherwood, Mary B.
> '*Pilgrim: A biography of William Brewster*' Great Oak Press, Virginia 1982

and the following websites:

Bassetlaw Museum and District
www.bassetlawmuseum.org.uk/projects/
www.bassetlaw.gov.uk/index/leisure_and_culture/local-history-and-heritage/**pilgrim-fathers**.htm

Mayflower History
www.mayflowerhistory.com/Passengers/**WilliamBrewster**.php -

Nottinghamshire Links
www.**pilgrimfathers**.visitnottingham.com/

Pilgrims and Plymouth
www.pilgrims.net/plymouth/history/

Pilgrim Fathers UK origins
www.**pilgrimfathers**origins.org/
Pilgrim Hall
www.pilgrimhall.org/**brewsterwilliam**records.htm
Rotherhithe links
www.stmaryrotherhithe.org/rotherhithe-and-the-**pilgrim**s.php
The ARIES Project at
www.captainjohnsmith.co.uk
The Pilgrim Archives in the Netherlands
www.**pilgrim**archives.nl/
William Brewster Society
www.mysite.verizon.net/**brewster**society/

Thanks

Many individuals have helped us with this book and we would like to thank them all.

In Gainsborough, UK:

Mrs Tracy Fulthorpe, Headteacher, Mr Peter Harrison, Miss Tracy Chapman and Mrs Elaine Jupp, Teachers and the Governors and Y5 and Y6 Pupils of the Parish Church Primary School, Gainsborough; Ms Karen Snell and Mr Jon Ducker of Gainsborough Old Hall; Mr Paul Howitt-Cowan of the Friends of the Old Hall

In Leiden, Holland

Dr Jeremy Bangs of the Leiden American Pilgrim Museum

In Lincolnshire, UK

Mrs Molly Burkett and Mrs Jayne Thompson of Barny Books; Mr Geoff Allinson and his team at Allinson Print; Mrs Jenny Haden of Julian Bower for her proof reading and patience when American history got in the way of other priorities.